McGWIRE & SOSA

A Season to Remember

JAMES PRELLER

Aladdin Paperbacks

To Mom,
for passing on the
love of the game

Catch!

First Aladdin Paperbacks edition November 1998

Text copyright ©1998 by James Preller

Aladdin Paperbacks
An imprint of Simon & Schuster
Children's Publishing Division
1230 Avenue of the Americas
New York, NY 10020

Dinger.

Tater.

Long Ball.

Bomb.

Four-bagger.

Goner.

Round-tripper.

Big Fly.

Goin' Yard.

Losing One.

Elvis Has Left the Building.

HOME RUN!

Whatever you call it, it's the most singular feat in all of sports. It thrills fans and captures the imagination. It's what baseball dreams are made of: Going…going…gone. One mighty sweep of lumber, then liftoff. The ball soars through the night sky and clears the wall. Fans leap to their feet. The park explodes in a wild din of stomps and cheers.

No record in all of sports has been more revered than Roger Maris's 61 homers, set in 1961, for the New York Yankees. Players have chased it—and failed—for thirty-seven years.

Until the magical season of 1998.

The summer of Sammy and Mac.

The questions were hurled before the first pitch of the season was thrown. Can this be the year when Roger Maris's record finally falls? And if so, who can do it?

Most observers turned to two people: Mark McGwire and Ken Griffey, Jr. McGwire because he'd been launching moonshots throughout his career—and he had come so close in 1997, belting 58 dingers. As for Ken Griffey, Jr., well, he slammed 56 round-trippers the previous season. And most everyone agreed: Mr. Griffey was quite simply the most magnificent player in the game.

"If someone gets to 50 by September 1, they have a shot down the stretch run."

—*Mark McGwire, during spring training*

Searching for likely record-breakers, few experts even considered the 200-pounder who patrols right field for the Chicago Cubs. Why should they? Clearly, Sammy Sosa was a great player, a former All-Star with a four-year, $42.5 million dollar contract. In the previous season, Slammin' Sammy ripped 36 home runs and drove in 119 runs. But he was always a free-swinger and a free spirit, wildly undisciplined at the plate, with a tendency to chase high fast balls and breaking balls in the dirt. He struck out a league-leading 174 times in 1997. Before the heroics of 1998, Sammy's greatest home run total was 40. Not a paltry number. But surely, Sosa was not in the same league as the likes of Griffey and McGwire.

Or so it seemed then, in the spring of 1998.

"Mark McGwire
is the man."
—Sammy Sosa

Even before his unfor-
gettable summer, Mark
McGwire was one of the
most respected figures in
all of professional sports.
A quiet man, McGwire car-
ried himself with calm and
dignity. His peers genuine-
ly liked him—and they
were awed by his ability.
At six-feet, five-inches and
250 pounds of chiseled
muscle, McGwire was a
portrait of pure power.

He looked every inch
"The Slugger."

Mark McGwire was born the second of five sons to John and Ginger McGwire, of Paloma, California. Growing up, Mark enjoyed a comfortable, middle-class life under the dry sun and manicured lawns of the

leagues in 1987 with the Oakland A's by hitting a rookie-season record 49 homers. Mark was a star on a team of stars, including all-time saves leader Dennis Eckersley, pitching ace Dave Stewart, and fellow "Bash Brother"

exactly 9 home runs each year. Depressed and tired of rehab, Mark almost retired from the game he loved.

But instead of hanging it up, Mark got focused. He hit the weight room with a vengeance. He set

Southern California suburbs. His father earned a good living as a dentist while his mother, Ginger, selflessly gave her time and energy to a variety of causes.

At age ten, a pudgy Mark McGwire homered in his first Little League at bat. He's been wearing out pitchers ever since. After a great college career, highlighted with a starring turn for the 1984 U.S. Olympic team, Mark burst into the major

Jose Canseco. Oakland rolled to the World Series three years in a row.

But in 1991, things went terribly wrong. Mark's average dipped to an embarrassing .201. He hit a mortal 22 home runs. Mark rebounded with a solid season in '92, but then the wheels—almost literally—came off. A series of foot injuries limited him to just 74 games over the next two seasons, 1993–94. He managed

new goals—as a player and as a person. By the time of his trade to the St. Louis Cardinals late in the 1997 season, Mark was all the way back. Over two seasons, he smashed 110 home runs. Mark loved St. Louis—and the fans of St. Louis loved him right back. In the spring of 1998, Mark seemed poised for greatness, ready to make the run of his life. He was shooting for the history books.

"**Holes remain in [Sosa's] swing, both up and in, and down and away. Now 29, this may be as good as he gets.**"
—*Taken from The Scouting Notebook 1998, a preseason scouting report published by STATS, Inc.*

Meanwhile, in the Chicago Cubs spring training camp, Sammy Sosa was hard at work. Under the guidance of hitting coach Jeff Pentland, Sammy was ready to make some adjustments. He lowered his hands, shortened his swing, and started thinking about hitting to the opposite field. Importantly, he made a serious effort to become more selective at the plate. Coach Pentland later told a group of reporters, "From the day Sammy arrived at spring training, we went to work. He came here with a smile on his face, and it never left."

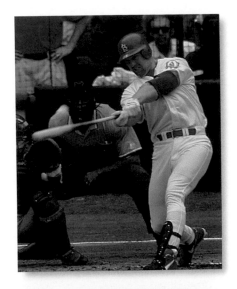

PHOTO: ALLSPORT/Vincent La Foret

Mark McGwire began the season with a smash. Then another…and another…and another. Just like that, 1-2-3-4. On April 4, Mark McGwire—wielding his 33-ounce, 34 ½-inch bat like an axe in the hands of a lumberjack—tied Willie Mays's 1971 record for consecutive home run games to open the season. Four games, four home runs. Fans across the country began to think:

He just might do it.

Big Mac continued his blistering pace through the early months of the season. To say he hit home runs is an understatement.

drove a ball 550 feet. It was the longest home run ever hit in Busch Stadium. Heck, it was easily the longest home run *anybody* would

He hit rockets. He sent balls into orbit. His high, rainbow shots became legend. On May 8th, he smashed No. 20, passing Babe Ruth to become the fastest player in major league history to reach 400 homers. Mark did it in 4,726 at-bats—128 faster than the great Bambino.

Hitting against Livan Hernandez of the Florida Marlins on May 16, Mark

hit all season, *anywhere*. The astonishing numbers kept piling up. By May 24, McGwire sat atop the home run leader board with 24, far outdistancing Roger Maris's record-setting pace. Ken Griffey lagged behind, tagging 18 over the same period. Sammy Sosa had only 9. But Sam the man was about to go on one of the hottest hot streaks in baseball history.

"We respect each other tremendously. Here's two guys from two different countries who have great sportsmanship, really admire each other and really pull for each other." — Mark McGwire

PHOTO: ALLSPORT/Elsa Hasch

For power hitters, home runs are like bananas. They come in bunches. A guy goes on a tear and it's bing, bing, bing. He rips off three in one day, six in a week. But rarely can a slugger stay that hot for an entire month. Thing is, somebody forgot to tell Sammy Sosa. From May 25 to June 21, Sammy slammed 21 home runs in the 22 games he played. He set a one-month record with 20 "see-ya-laters" in June, including the three he hit on June 15 against poor Cal Eldred of the Montreal Expos.

The chase was on. At the All-Star break, Mark McGwire had tied Reggie Jackson's 1969 record of 37 homers by the summer-time classic. Seattle Mariner Ken Griffey, Jr. was close behind with 35 round-trippers. Sammy Sosa, seemingly coming from nowhere, had closed the margin with 33 of his own. The "Maris Watch" had begun in earnest. But there was still a long, long way to go.

Despite Sammy Sosa's furious storm of home runs, his performance barely registered with the American public. All eyes were fixed on McGwire. Hungry for quotes, reporters swarmed the Cardinals slugger in ravenous masses. The media was in a feeding frenzy—and everyone wanted a piece of Big Mac. Huge press conferences became routine each time McGwire and the Cards visited a new city. Mark grew weary of the questions. Sometimes it showed. The pressure began to build.

But Sammy Sosa kept crowding into the spotlight reserved for McGwire. On August 11, the nation awoke to the startling news that Sosa had tied McGwire at 46 bombs each. Fans around the country could no longer ignore the presence of Sammy Sosa. They soon learned what the Chicago fans already knew: Sammy was a one-of-a-kind personality. He was a class act all the way.

Sammy Sosa grew up in San Pedro de Macoris in the Dominican Republic. His family was poor, even by the standards of a poor country. His father died when Sammy was seven. He watched as his widowed mother, Lucrecya, worked long hours as a

maid to provide for him, his four brothers, and two sisters. Sammy slept on a dirt floor. He sold oranges, washed cars, and shined shoes to help his family. His first baseball glove was fashioned from an inside-out milk carton. For a bat, Sammy grabbed a tree branch. A rolled-up sock was the ball.

He was blessed with talent. Sammy could play the game. It soon became clear that baseball offered him and his family an escape from the grinding cycle of poverty. At Sammy's first big league tryout, a scout for the Texas Rangers scribbled "looks malnourished" in his notepad. Then he signed the skinny, smiling, 150-pound kid—who didn't speak three words of English—to a modest $3,500 contract.

When better money came after he arrived in the major leagues, Sammy did what was only natural. He built a new home for his mother. Sammy explained, "In the Dominican, family is different....It is my duty to support them. I have money now, but I'm still poor. I'm the same guy I was back then. You never lose who you are, and that boy shining shoes is still who I am."

How could the people of America not fall in love with a guy like that?

"Pressure was to me when I didn't have food on the table. Now that I am here this is nothing."
— *Sammy Sosa*

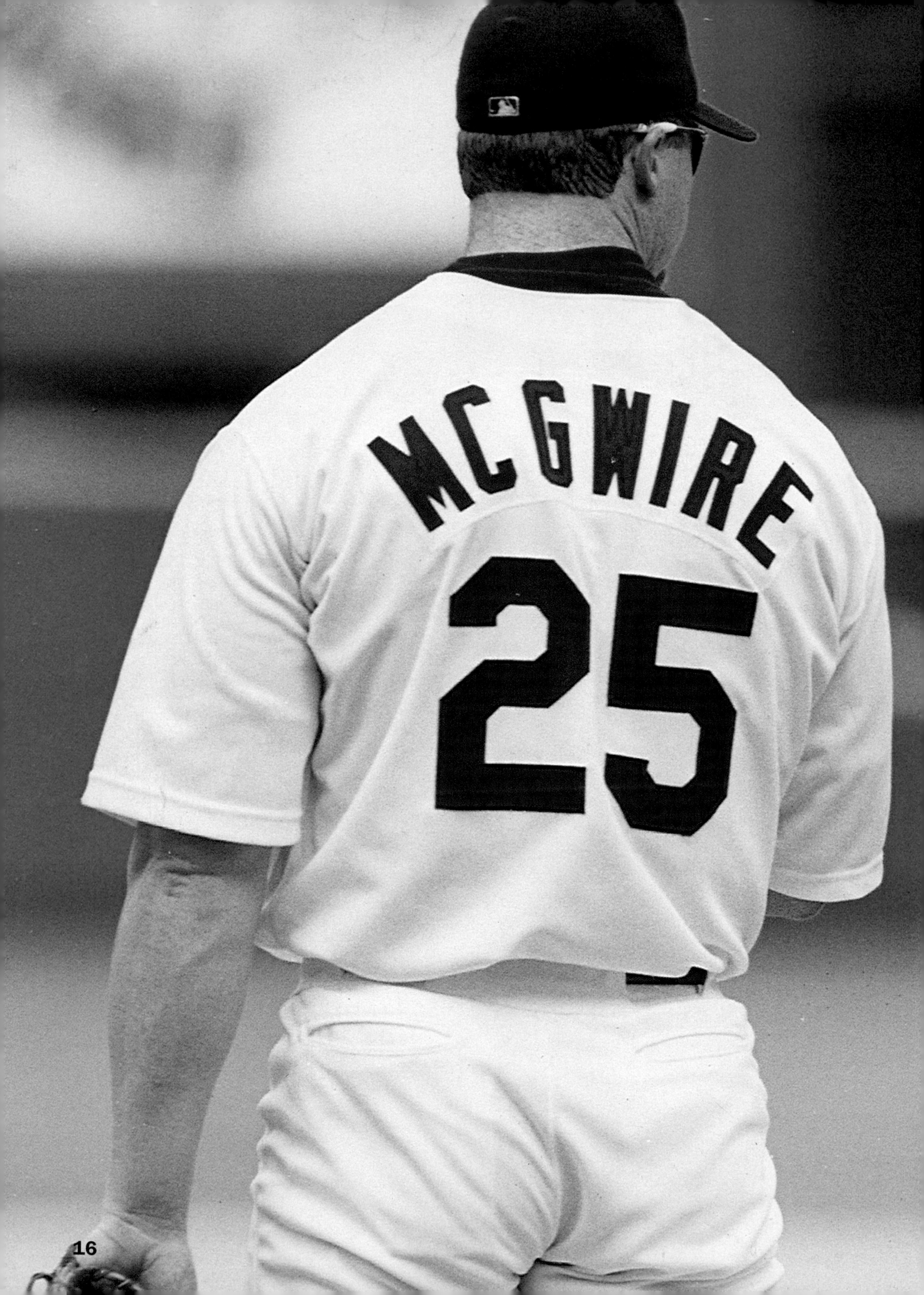
MCGWIRE
25

17

When Griffey hit a home run drought in early August, the great home run race became a two-man duel. And in many ways, it provided a study in contrasts. Native son McGwire, the Olympian, the All-American boy, battling the rags-to-riches immigrant, Sammy Sosa, who would repeatedly tell anyone who cared to listen: "I love this country."

There were other differences beyond economic backgrounds.

Sosa's Cubs were locked in a fierce wild-card chase with the Mets and Giants. For the Cardinals, wins and losses failed to matter; a below-.500 club, they were hopelessly mired in a disappointing season. McGwire was their saving grace.

At the plate, Big Mac featured a classic, compact swing. He disdainfully picked over the pitches, rejecting many like bad fruit at the market. He led the league in walks by an enormous margin. Sammy, even with his new-found selectivity, was still a hacker at heart. Five inches smaller and fifty pounds lighter than McGwire, Sammy derived his power from lightning-quick hands and perfect timing as hips turned, the torso rotated, and bat met ball.

"They've carried the sport all summer."

– Padres outfielder Tony Gwynn, speaking of McGwire and Sosa

It must be said: McGwire handled the daily pressures with dignity and grace. Yet he seemed burdened by it all, at times downright grumpy, once even complaining in mid-August of feeling like a "caged animal." Sammy, on the other hand, just laughed and winked and wisecracked and laughed some more. He was having the time of his life, and Sammy would tell you so if you asked.

Confessed McGwire, "Sometimes when you think about the whole world watching you, that's a lot of pressure for just one person." But the divorced father who lived by himself in a St. Louis hotel wasn't alone any longer. Now Mac had Sammy—and his load seemed lighter. On a road swing through Chicago, Big Mac got the chance to chat with Sammy. Mark enjoyed just feeling Sammy's joyful energy, hearing his contagious laughter. Immediately, Mark appeared more relaxed. He even started flashing a smile that was almost, well, *Sosa-like*.

"It'd be great to talk to him. It would be so neat to go back to those days. But you know what? I'd guess he'd be a lot like me."
—Mark McGwire, speaking of Roger Maris

Roger Maris, 1961

PHOTO: AP/WIDE WORLD PHOTO

As the homers kept coming—48, 49, 50, 51—thoughts inevitably turned to Roger Maris. With Big Mac's respect for baseball lore, he was keenly aware of the Yankee slugger's bittersweet 1961 record-breaking season.

But to talk of Maris, you've first got to understand Babe Ruth and what he meant to baseball. The game's first superstar, Babe was a pioneer. He reinvented the game by charting new boundaries for power hitters. Ruth was loved by the fans. No, he was more than loved—Babe was a giant, bigger than the game itself. In the baseball world, there was Babe Ruth, and then there was everybody else. His 1927 record of 60 home runs stood like a mountain for thirty-four years, an imposing Everest that could never be climbed.

Roger Maris—a quiet man from Fargo, North Dakota—was an unlikely candidate to break Ruth's

mark. Going into the 1961 season, Maris had a season homer high of 39. Most thought that if anyone was going to challenge the record, it would be either teammate Mickey Mantle or

Babe Ruth, 1931

PHOTO: ALLSPORT/Hulton Deitsch

Willie Mays of the San Francisco Giants.

But all season long, the 200-pound Yankee right fielder steadily hit home runs. The nearer he got to the record, the greater the pressure. Many fans and even teammates did not want him to overtake Ruth. Maris received hate mail from fans. He heard verbal abuse from the stands. It seemed to

Maris as if the whole world was rooting against him.

Roger responded by losing his hair, losing weight, and becoming withdrawn and bitter. Still, he continued his assault on the record. On October 1, the last game of the season, before a sparse, strangely indifferent crowd of 23,154 fans, Roger Maris broke Babe Ruth's record by hitting his 61st home run.

Two years later, on that exact date, Mark McGwire was born.

Before the game on September 8, 1998, Mark McGwire met with Hall of Fame officials. They brought with them Roger Maris's bat—the one that smacked No. 61 off Tracy Stallard. Thrilled, Big Mac held the historic bat, took a few cuts, and rolled the barrel over his heart. He said, "Roger, I hope you're with me tonight."

The rest, as they say, is history.

You couldn't have asked for a better setting. With McGwire poised at 49 round-trippers, the Cardinals came into New York to play a pair of double-headers against the Mets. It wasn't lost on McGwire that he was playing across town from Yankee Stadium, the House That Ruth Built. The same stadium where Maris hit his record-breaker in '61.

First came, of course, The Amazing Mark McGwire Talent Show. In other words, batting practice. That's right, *batting practice*. Usually a yawner as far as fans are concerned—unless Big Mac happens to be near the bat rack. Then it becomes an event, something to bring the grandkids to, just so they can one day tell *their* grandchildren about it. Hours before game time, Shea Stadium was packed with thousands of eager fans. McGwire made sure they got their money's worth, launching one pitch after another across awesome lengths.

In the seventh inning of the first game, August 20, Mark lifted a big fly for No. 50. In a rare show of emotion, Mark pumped his fist rounding first. The New York crowd, like all the others around baseball, stood and cheered.

For a long, long time.

As well they should. After all, McGwire was the biggest thing to come to New York since Godzilla. And besides, he put on a better show: Mac hit No. 51 in the second game.

PHOTO: ALLSPORT/Andy Lyons

"What he has done for St. Louis and the rest of the country has been incredible. Years from now, people will talk about Mark being one of the greatest."
—Baseball Hall of Famer Stan Musial

PHOTO: ALLSPORT/Stephen Dunn

Sammy and Mac kept playing their private game of "top-this." McGwire usually led by a couple, then balls, with ink that could be seen only under infrared light, for Mark's at-bats. This was to authenti- playing the Cubs. Steve Trachsel was on the mound for Chicago. Little did he realize he was

Sammy would reel off a few bombs to tie. Then on September 1, Mark hit No.'s 56 and 57. Then next day, two more: 58 and 59. Now it was just a matter of time before the record fell.

When the day came, September 8, in St. Louis, Major League Baseball was ready. They used special cate the historic ball that was to become No. 62 and, hopefully, come to reside in the sleepy village of Cooperstown, home of the Baseball Hall of Fame.

The fans were ready, too—it seemed like everybody had a flash camera, desperate to capture the magic. The Cards were about to become the answer to a trivia question. Sammy Sosa was in right field when McGwire lined a screaming rocket into the left field corner. Just like that: The most legendary record in sports, one that had stood for thirty-seven years, was shattered.

In the moments after the historic blast, in the blur of euphoria, Mark McGwire somehow managed to do everything right. At home plate, Mark lifted his son Matthew into the air and held him tight.

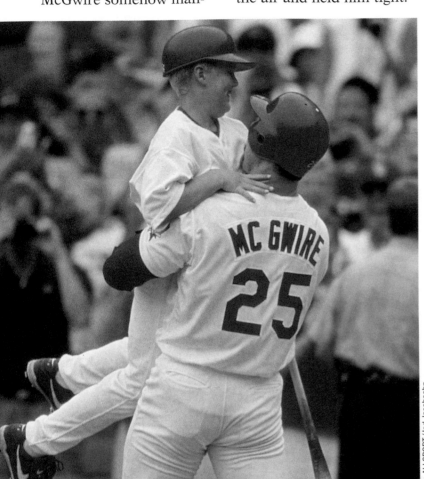

PHOTO: ALLSPORT/Jed Jacobsohn

In fact, he pretty much hugged anyone with a pulse. Even Sammy Sosa raced in from the outfield to hug his friend. Mark paid tribute to his parents, then climbed into the stands to honor the Maris family, who had flown in to witness the event. Amidst the emotional celebration, the game was forgotten.

The record was broken. And it felt, for a brief moment, like the great race had been won.

But it wasn't over yet. Not by a long shot. Or more accurately, not by *several* long shots—most of which came off the streaking bat of Sammy Sosa. The man from San Pedro de Macoris wasn't done yet.

"It's an absolutely incredible feeling. I can honestly say I did it."
—Mark McGwire, after hitting No. 62

Maybe Mark McGwire relaxed. Because for one full week, he didn't hit another home run. It was time enough for Sam the man to go yard four more times. On September 13, he sent a 480-foot blast over

the ivy-covered wall and into an alley behind Waveland Avenue.

Home run No. 62!

Maris's longstanding record had been passed twice in a week. Mark McGwire and Sammy Sosa were tied at 62 with two weeks of the season left to play. On September 25, they were tied again at 66 each. You could count the games left on your fingers. The two epic sluggers—in one of the greatest athletic competitions of all time— were no longer chasing a statistic in a dusty record book. They were chasing each other.

McGwire clubbed 4 home runs in his last 7 at-bats to reach an astonishing 70 homers for the season, topping Sammy Sosa to become baseball's new king of swing.

But don't feel too bad for Mr. Sosa. He got what he wanted after all—the trip to the playoffs he so richly deserved.

Smiling brightly, Mark McGwire concluded, "It's absolutely amazing. It blows me away."

As fans, we knew the feeling.

"Sammy! Sammy! Sammy!"

—40,846 fans, screaming as one, at Wrigley Field on the day Sammy Sosa tied Mark McGwire at 62.

SOSA HRs

Home runs, by number, hit by Sammy Sosa of the Chicago Cubs with date, opposing team and pitcher.

HR	Date, Team/Pitcher	HR	Date, Team/Pitcher
1	Apr. 4, Expos/Valdes	36	July 17, MARLINS/Ojala
2	Apr. 11, EXPOS/Telford	37	July 22, Expos, Batista
3	Apr. 15, METS/Reed	38	July 26, Mets, Reed
4	Apr. 23, Padres/Miceli	39	July 27, DIAMONDBACKS/Blair
5	Apr. 24, DODGERS/Valdes	40	July 27, DIAMONDBACKS/Embree
6	Apr. 27, PADRES/Hamilton	41	July 28, DIAMONDBACKS/Wolcott
7	May 3, Cardinals/Politte	42	July 31, Rockies/Wright
8	May 16, REDS/Sullivan	43	Aug. 5, Diamondbacks/Benes
9	May 22, BRAVES/Maddux	44	Aug. 8, CARDINALS/Croushore
10	May 25, BRAVES/Millwood	45	Aug. 10, GIANTS/Ortiz
11	May 25, BRAVES/Cather	46	Aug. 10, GIANTS/Brock
12	May 27, Phillies/Winston	47	Aug. 16, ASTROS/Bergman
13	May 27, Phillies/Gomes	48	Aug. 19, Cardinals/Bottenfield
14	June 1, Marlins/Dempster	49	Aug. 21, Giants/Hershiser
15	June 1, Marlins/Henriquez	50	Aug. 23, Astros/Lima
16	June 3, Marlins/Hernandez	51	Aug. 23, Astros/Lima
17	June 5, White Sox/Parque	52	Aug. 26, REDS/Tomko
18	June 6, White Sox/Castillo	53	Aug. 28, ROCKIES/Thomson
19	June 7, White Sox/Baldwin	54	Aug. 30, ROCKIES/Kile
20	June 8, TWINS/Hawkins	55	Aug. 31, Reds/Tomko
21	June 13, PHILLIES/Portugal	56	Sept. 2, Reds/Bere
22	June 15, Expos/Eldred	57	Sept. 4, PIRATES/Schmidt
23	June 15, Expos/Eldred	58	Sept. 5, PIRATES/Lawrence
24	June 15, Expos/Eldred	59	Sept. 11, Brewers/Pulsipher
25	June 17, Brewers/Patrick	60	Sept. 12, Brewers/D.L. Santos
26	June 19, Phillies/Loewer	61	Sept. 13, Brewers/Patrick
27	June 19, Phillies/Loewer	62	Sept. 13, Brewers/Plunk
28	June 20, Phillies/Beech	63	Sept. 16, Padres/Boeringer
29	June 20, Phillies/Borland	64	Sept. 23, BREWERS/Roque
30	June 21, Phillies/Green	65	Sept. 23, BREWERS/Henderson
31	June 24, TIGERS/Greisinger	66	Sept. 25, ASTROS/Lima
32	June 25, TIGERS/Moehler		
33	June 30, Diamondbacks/Embree		
34	July 9, BREWERS/Juden		
35	July 10, BREWERS/Karl		

Home teams in ALL CAPS

Sosa's 1998 Batting Statistics

G	AB	R	H	2B	3B	HR	RBI	BB	SO	SB	CS	OBP	SLG	AVG
159	643	134	198	20	0	66	158	73	171	18	9	.377	.647	.308

McGWIRE HRs

Home runs, by number, hit by Mark McGwire of the St. Louis Cardinals with date, opposing team and pitcher.

HR	Date, Team/Pitcher	HR	Date, Team/Pitcher
1	Mar. 31, Dodgers/Martinez	36	June 27, TWINS/Trombley
2	Apr. 2, Dodgers/Lankford	37	June 30, Royals/Rusch
3	Apr. 3, Padres/Langston	38	July 11, Astros/Wagner
4	Apr. 4, Padres/Wengert	39	July 12, Astros/Bergman
5	Apr. 14, Diamondbacks/Suppan	40	July 12, Astros/Elarton
6	Apr. 14, Diamondbacks/Suppan	41	July 17, Dodgers/Bohannon
7	Apr. 14, Diamondbacks/Manuel	42	July 17, Dodgers/Osuna
8	Apr. 17, Phillies/Whiteside	43	July 20, PADRES/Boeringer
9	Apr. 21, EXPOS/Moore	44	July 26, Rockies/Thomson
10	Apr. 25, PHILLIES/Spradlin	45	July 28, BREWERS/Myers
11	Apr. 30, CUBS/Pisciotta	46	Aug. 8, Cubs/Clark
12	May 1, CUBS/Beck	47	Aug. 11, Mets/Jones
13	May 8, METS/Reed	48	Aug. 19, CUBS/Karchner
14	May 12, Brewers/Wagner	49	Aug 19, CUBS/Mulholland
15	May 14, Braves/Millwood	50	Aug. 20, METS/Blair
16	May 16, Marlins/Hernandez	51	Aug. 20, METS/Reed
17	May 18, Marlins/Sanchez	52	Aug. 22, PIRATES/Cordova
18	May 19, PHILLIES/Green	53	Aug. 23, PIRATES/Rincon
19	May 19, PHILLIES/Green	54	Aug. 26, Marlins/Speier
20	May 19, PHILLIES/Gomes	55	Aug. 30, Braves/Martinez
21	May 22, Giants/Gardner	56	Sept. 1, MARLINS/Hernandez
22	May 23, Giants/Rodriquez	57	Sept. 1, MARLINS/Pall
23	May 23, Giants/Johnstone	58	Sept. 2, MARLINS/Edmondson
24	May 24, Giants/Nen	59	Sept. 2, MARLINS/Stanifer
25	May 25, Rockies/Thomson	60	Sept. 5, Reds/Reyes
26	May 29, PADRES/Miceli	61	Sept. 7, Cubs/Morgan
27	May 30, PADRES/Ashby	62	Sept. 8, Cubs/Trachsel
28	June 5, Giants/Hershiser	63	Sept. 15, Pirates/Christensen
29	June 8, WHITE SOX/Bere	64	Sept. 18, Brewers/Roque
30	June 10, WHITE SOX/Parque	65	Sept. 20, Brewers/Karl
31	June 12, DIAMONDBACKS/Benes	66	Sept. 25, Expos/Bennett
32	June 17, ASTROS/Lima	67	Sept. 26, Expos/Hermanson
33	June 18, ASTROS/Reynolds	68	Sept. 26, Expos/Bullinger
34	June 24, INDIANS/Wright	69	Sept. 27, Expos/Thurman
35	June 25, INDIANS/Burba	70	Sept. 27, Expos/Pavano

Home teams in ALL CAPS

McGwire's 1998 Batting Statistics

G	AB	R	H	2B	3B	HR	RBI	BB	SO	SB	CS	OBP	SLG	AVG
155	509	130	152	21	0	70	147	162	155	1	0	.470	.752	.299

"I wish that every player in the game could have the experience I'm having."

—Mark McGwire

Mark McGwire and Sammy Sosa. Their names will be linked forever. Because nobody—*nobody*—has ever hit more home runs in a season than these two guys.

Because beyond the moon shots and screaming liners, beyond the bombs and dingers and long balls, beyond this spectacle of greatness, we'll have this: a shining model of what competition is really all about. McGwire and Sosa.

Big Mac and Sammy. Two men bringing out the best in each other. Two gracious, honorable heroes in an age when heroes are hard to come by. Before our eyes these two athletes—loving fathers both—defined the word "sportsman" for a new generation of fans.

Sure, maybe there's a single name beside a statistic in a record book. Maybe the record will last, maybe it won't. Maybe

there's a winner in this race for the ages, but he's surely not alone. Because in the unforgettable summer of 1998, *everybody wins*: McGwire, Sosa, the millions of fans who cheered them to greatness. Everybody goes home happy, proud for being just a small part of it, glad to have been invited to ride the wave, thinking: *Geez, wasn't that something. Wasn't that really something.*

3924